Colour
Your Way Through
Yellowknife

Copyright 2015 by MadlieWords

All rights reserved. No part of this book may be
reproduced in any form without permission
in writing from the author/publisher.

ISBN: 978-0-9949564-0-8

Designed by Elizabeth Purchase and Tanya Leontyeva

Created in Yellowknife, NT Canada

This Book Belongs To:

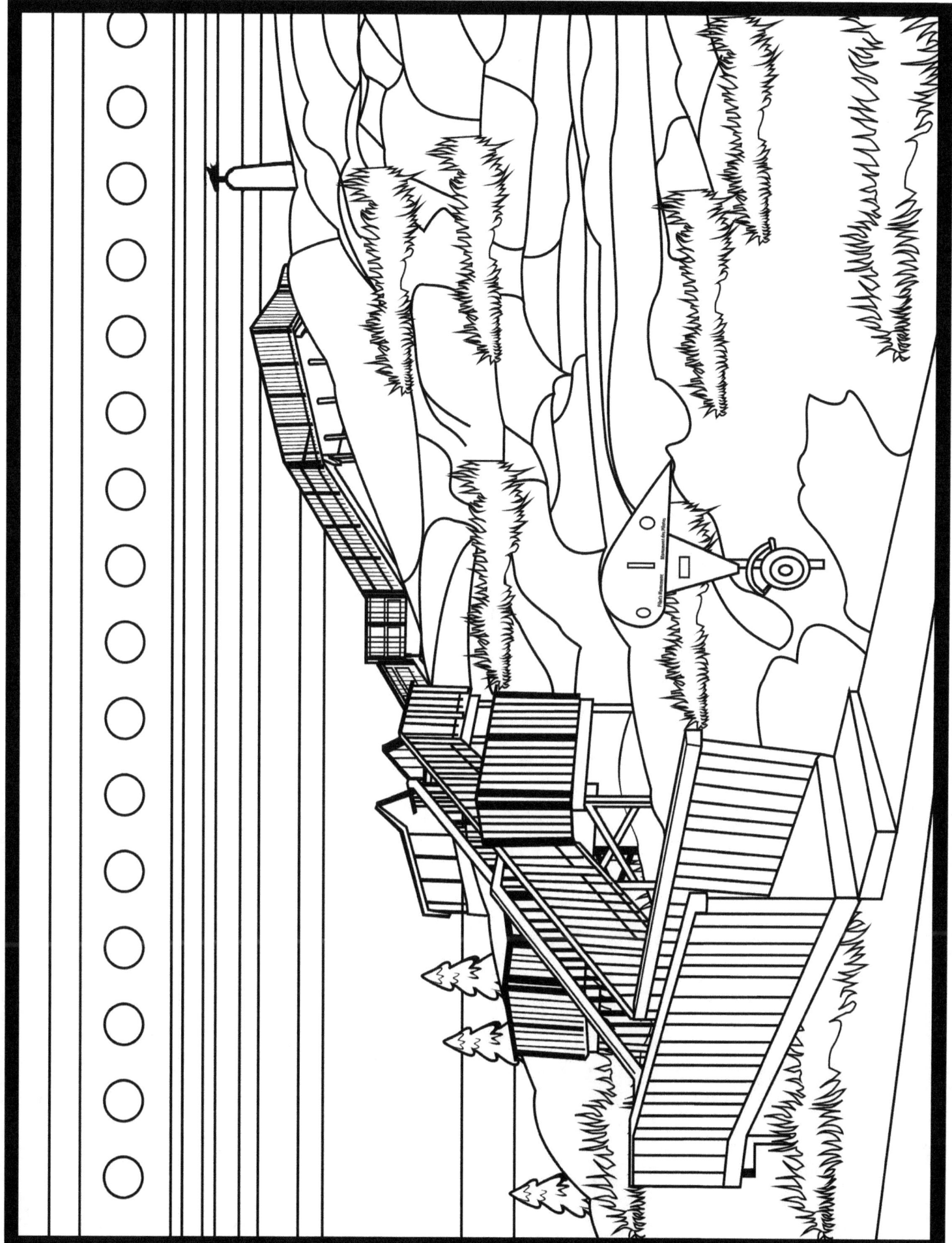

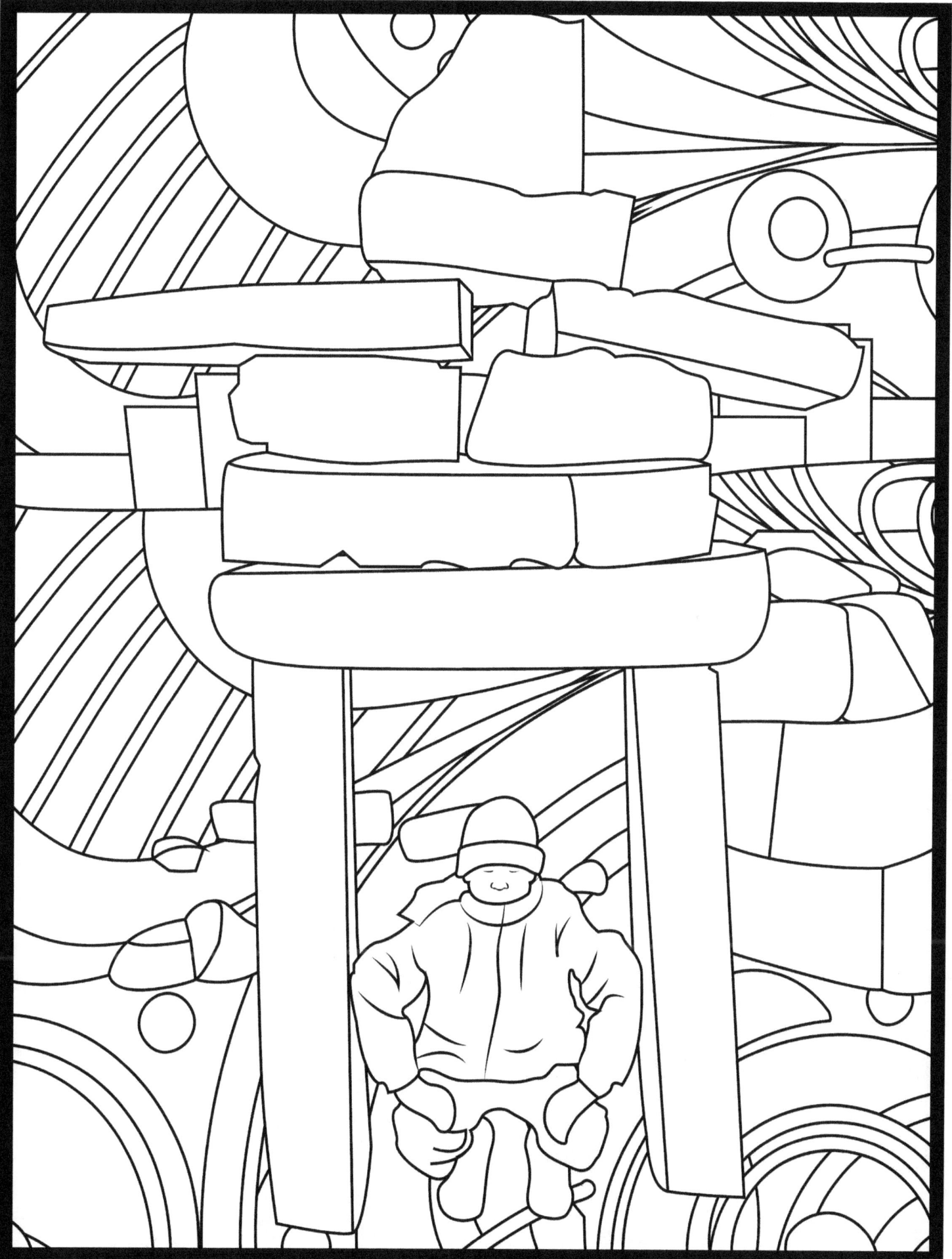

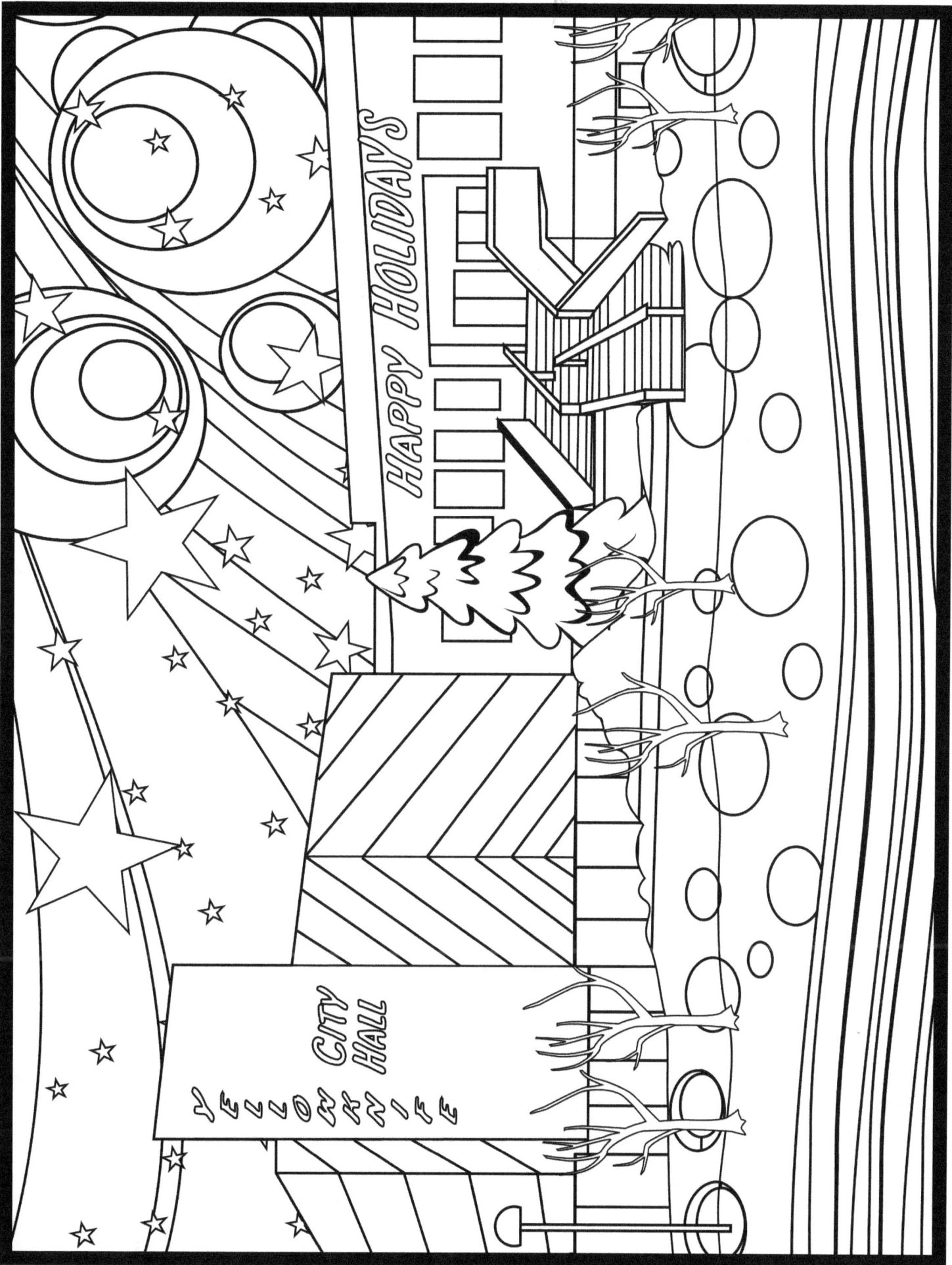

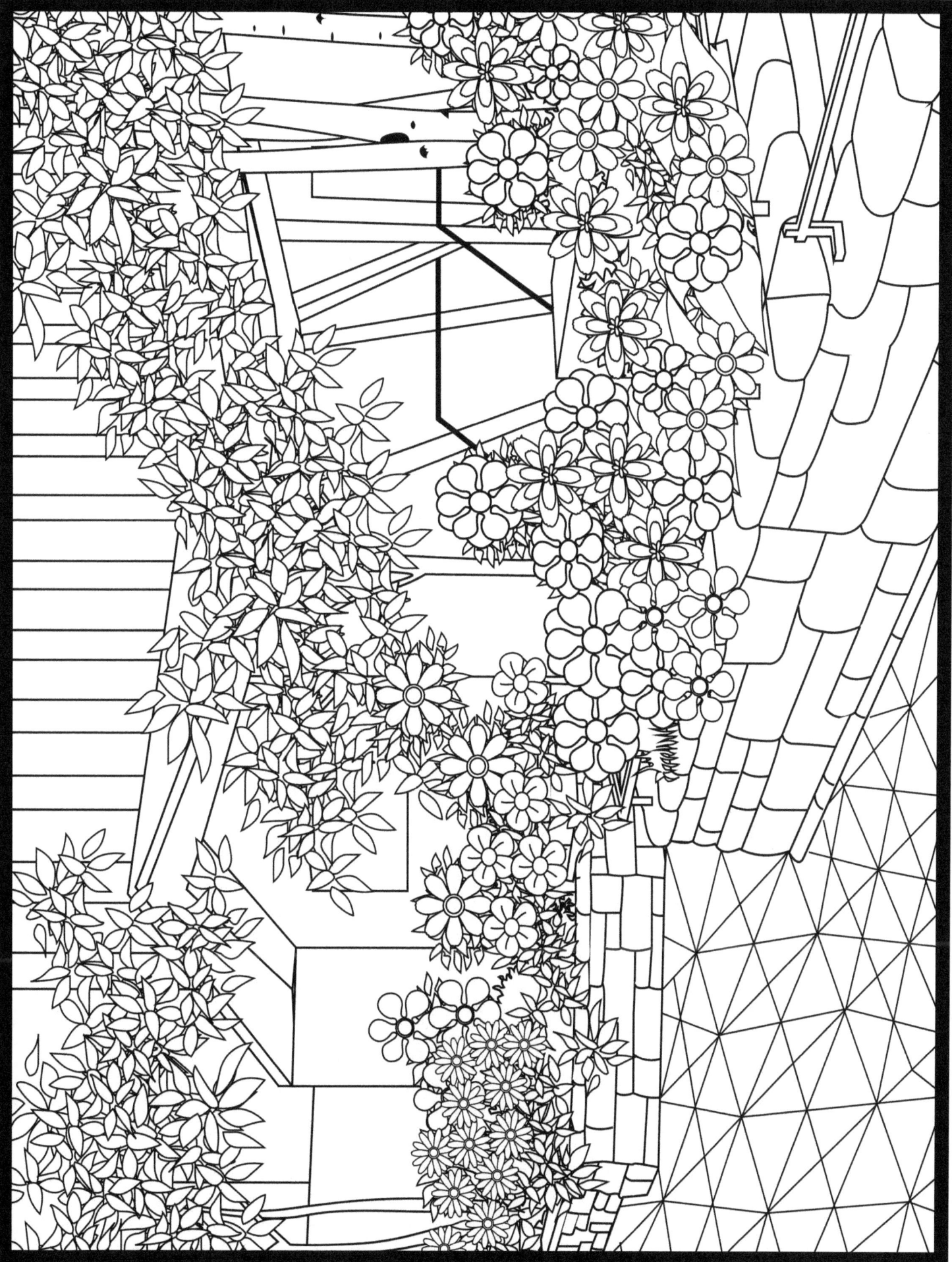

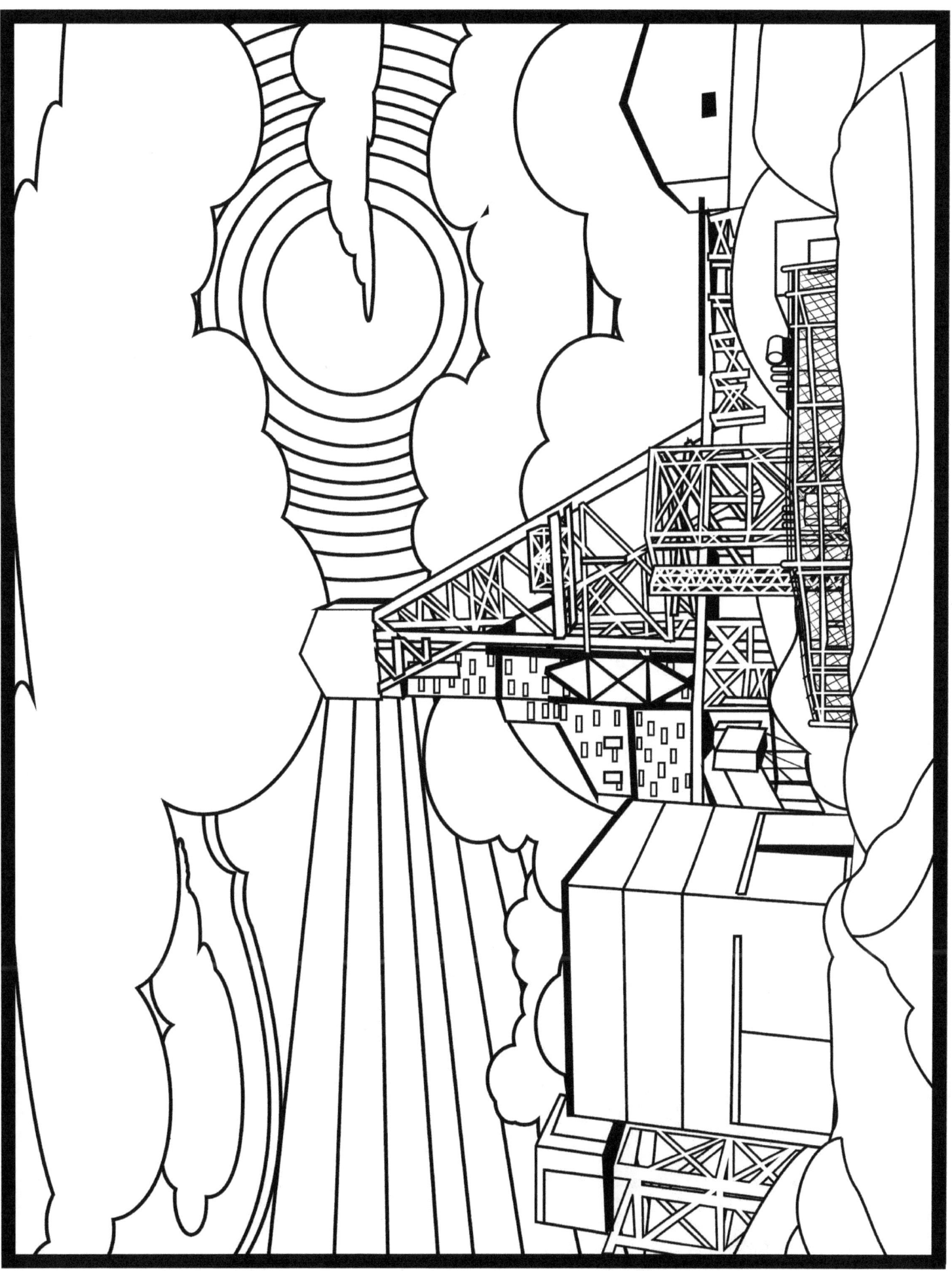

This book is dedicated to
my Auntie Lin

Thank you for your
love and support!

By Elizabeth Purchase
www.madliewords.ca

www.ingramcontent.com/pod-product-compliance
Lightning Source LLC
Chambersburg PA
CBHW081351040426
42450CB00015B/3389